How to Be a World Leader

Visit the site for more information on books by Tyler Moses and to be informed of free promotions!

We all have an element of crazy and power hunger can take over the good intentions of most but what does it really take to be a World Leader read on to find out!

Please see other books by

Tyler Moses

How to Get a Rich Woman

How to Be a Golddigger

The Truth About Getting Old

Please see other Titles from

ARYLA PUBLISHING

Children's Books

The Body Goo Series

The Billy Series

Adult Books

Self Help Books

Diet and Wellbeing

Table of Contents

Chapter 1: Introduction

Welcome to the year 2017. The world has changed.

The last few years have seen political developments that all the wisest heads of the Western world completely failed to predict – journalists, politicians and rich billionaires alike. And the people who usually have a habit of making out they know what's going on and why.

The election of Donald Trump as President of the United States – leader of the Free World! – sticks out most obviously in this respect. All the so-called experts spent months ridiculing the very idea. Indeed, even the very idea that he might become the Republican candidate seemed a far-fetched notion and neither were they shrewd enough to learn their lesson once proven wrong on that score. Following that shock, they continued to imagine that matters could not get any weirder, settling for what they saw as a pretty safe assumption that Hilary Clinton would be the one to take office.

What none of these people took seriously was not only the caliber of the presidential candidate but also the will of the people and their ability to make it count. What bonds existed between the public and media consciousness appear to have been severed, making for quite an unpredictable modern world. The head doesn't appear to know what the body is doing and so President Trump's election is one of a series of results that have the Western world especially struggling to get a grip. Add to this the United Kingdom's decision to leave the European Union, as well as France's election of President Macron, who seemed to rise from nowhere, and we have a phenomenon that onlookers have taken to explaining as 'anti-establishment' voting. That is what they're calling it, but the truth is that having a name for it doesn't take away the reality that no one really has a definitive answer as to what is going on. In this case, thinking up clever terms in order to look wise after the event does not cover up the fact that the so-called experts are clueless.

Be that as it may, one upshot is that the corridors of powers have suddenly become more versatile than ever before. No longer will the next world leader be vetted and mentored to the point where every ounce of personality and individualism has been purged from their soul by some political party. Right now, the people who usually make these decisions behind closed doors are feeling powerless, knowing that the candidate they would like to tailor for the position might just be kicked unceremoniously into obscurity by an electorate that is not playing ball.

Who knows? You might be able to become a world leader, no matter what your background. Did you drop out of high school? No worries! Money is what talks – money and social media these days and anyone who is self-centered enough to be a world leader is capable of being self-centered enough to play the gold digger in order to blackmail their way into office.

After all, if Donald Trump can do it, so can you and I!

In fact, keeping 'the wrong sort' out all this time has always been something of a construct of the political classes, but history shows that they can only ever keep power artificial for so long. Times of fluctuation and versatility are just as common as those of stagnation, so you may be surprised to know that many famous – and infamous names – came from nowhere to become the ones running the show. Julius Caesar, for example, was once a complete unknown when, back in 60 B.C.E, he rose to power by forming strategic alliances with wealthy people so that he could buy his way into ruling an empire. Lack of money didn't hold him back and neither did it Adolf Hitler, whose ability to engage with the masses by flattering a sense of national pride proved fatal for so many. Perhaps this is why now is the real time to consider being someone that has a say, lest another agent of destruction beat us to the public's affections.

Let's keep this honest, however, as without candidness we will understand nothing. This is not a noble pursuit. We may pomp and swagger when reaching the world stage in order to flatter ourselves that we are the incarnation of nobility, but we are seeking to be the complete opposite. We are connivers, usurpers, liars and traitors; these are the tools of our trade and, if we learn how to use them opportunistically – all the while pretending to be something else – their application can bring us great success.

In order to do this, however, we need to be brutally honest about our worldview. No more thinking that lower classes are the 'salt of the earth' or flattering yourself that you care about their liberties. The lower classes are, for the most part, poorly educated, have stinted life perspectives and a fragile grasp of political issues. Whether you want to be a good or bad leader – and by good we mean not cause the demise of millions of people (everything is relative) – the general population are your cattle. You need to dangle the right carrot or piece of hay to get them from the one field they are idly grazing in, occasionally looking up to pull faces at passersby by as if they are capable of having an outlook on the world, into your own field. It's when they amble through those gates, under the illusion that they know what they are doing, when they become yours. In this strange and silly game, those who have the more sheep standing in their field get to rule the world. Even the odd smart sheep has to stand somewhere, so no need to get too carried away with flattering their intellect. You merely need to show them that your rivals have even less appeal than you actually do.

We'll delve further into how all this is possible but, to start with, just be sure not to let any of your usual hang-ups hold you back. The most powerful man in the world right now closely resembles an orange duck, so there is something to be said for acting confident and self-assured even if you have absolutely no visual appeal to back it up with. Most of this game is an illusion; a performance. If you have good looks they can come in useful of course, as I'm sure they have for Canadian prime minister, Justin Trudeau, or the newly elected French president, Emmanuel Macron, for example. They are the darlings of world leaders at the moment, but is it so far-fetched to imagine they have had to charm themselves into some rich women's panties on their way to the top? Call me cynical if you like, but I am highly suspicious of their butter-wouldn't-melt smiles.

Whatever your abilities, the key is to apply yourself in a way that is effective in getting doors open. Men and women alike can play this game – don't let Hilary Clinton's failure put you off. The UK's Conservative Party is a weird example of how toffee-nosed upper class men (of whom you will come across a lot of in power) have a strange fascination about being politically dominated by a woman. There's something sadomasochistic and Freudian going on that causes them to embrace having someone who looks like their old childhood nanny stand in their midst and giving the orders. It is a subversion of the conservative way that would usually be overly obsessed with male assertiveness. The truth is that they love the irony of something against the norm leading the way, as if somewhere in the mystery lies a secret recipe for rule – the magic potion they all want to sip of.

Indeed, they fall for this imagined aura so easily that, when it came to the chance of electing a second female leader (the Conservatives have never really been happy since Margaret Thatcher left) they went straight for Theresa May without actually checking that she had any talent for the role whatsoever. A year later, in a snap election she had the wisdom to call in order to increase their majority, she in fact lost the party's majority, after an election campaign in which she achieved nothing other than proving to the electorate that she was a bad choice.

As you can see, much of this game is pretty farcical. Shakespeare could have written it up better than me, but he would have actually been too noble to go one step further and explore how you can put yourself in their place. I am not so noble, so let's embark on a journey that will give you the necessary tools to trick the world into thinking you are the one for the job.

"The great masses of the people will more easily fall victims to a big lie than to a small one." – Adolf Hitler

Chapter 2: Examples of World Leaders

Learning from what has occurred before us remains crucial for anyone who wants to rule. Don't assume that the tools and techniques have changed just because we are in the age of TV and the Internet. All that has changed is the means and the presentation, but the tactics are the same even if, in the Western world for the most part, they are now considerably less bloody. The Romans, the Babylonians, the Byzantines, the Persians and the Greeks, all one-time great empires, all throve on tools like propaganda, alliance-building, diplomacy, negotiation and coercion. These are weapons of power regardless of whether your intentions are good or not. You need to learn from the best to become the most deceitful and manipulative politician around. Don't worry if history bores you to death. You only need an overview and the great thing about studying the past is that you can magnetize toward individuals whose methods strike a chord with you. In this chapter, we'll look at a few examples to see if any have an approach you are particularly keen to replicate.

So, let's take a trip down memory lane, into the days that everybody alive today is thankful they didn't have to live in. Back when wars were fought with fists and bayonets. To a time when leaders were decided through family lineage. I don't suppose you are likely to identify with many of these individuals on a personal level, but there are numerous examples of rulers who prove that, once upon the throne, the extent that you can get away with is staggering. Perhaps Ivan the Terrible is one of the best examples. He was Grand Prince of Moscow from 1533 to 1547 and then became "Tsar of All the Russians" until (thankfully) he finally died in 1584. He was born into his reign but, despite a Russian taste for uprisings and revolutions, he didn't show any paranoia about the security of his position. Indeed, nothing at all stopped him from acting bat shit crazy, ruling Russia in the same manner that a prison's toughest and most psychotic inmate might runs his gangs. Whenever he wasn't happy – for whatever reason – people died. He sent armies to slaughter entire villages just because he was having an off day, which kind of makes Vladimir Putin look like a sweet little pussycat.

You might think this kind of character belongs to the past, but there are modern day equivalents in terms of the pettiness and selfishness of their approach to power. Kim Jong-un, the leader of North Korea, is perhaps the closest to Ivan in nature. From what we see of him, he comes across as a child who throws a temper tantrum when he doesn't get a cookie. Someone we'd laugh at if it wasn't for the fact that he is absolute ruler of his country and developing a nuclear arsenal. Don't worry if you've had mental health issues; they shouldn't hold you back if Kim Jong-un is anything to go by. Fortunately, however, power isn't often handed down to spoilt brats in this way anymore, so you'll probably have to develop the ability to appear normal in some way, which is something that Kim Jong-un has yet to accomplish.

Actually, just to backtrack a little, the lineage scenario isn't that simple. Donald Trump, for example, is clearly in power today because he was born into a family with billions of dollars. He didn't inherit the Presidency but money talks and now we know that his connections were directing him to the White House long before he was even a sperm making its way up his mother's fallopian tube. By the time he could talk, his father's best friends were teaching him how to sniff out the best of Cuban cigars. He was that chubby ugly rich boy who camped out at the top of the biggest slide on the playground, requiring kids to perform special tasks before they could earn the right to go down. If you're the heir to a fortune, you act like the heir to a fortune. Bide your time, play as many bad hands as you want, and soon you'll be four divorces closer to becoming President of the United States.

What other examples are there of nutty leaders? So many countries to choose from. So many cultures and peoples. Oh yes!... Russia. Yes, a bit like the world news channels, we never want to go there but it's drawing our nose like an evil smell.

Russia has suffered through some nasty leaders. Joseph Stalin was the dictator of the Soviet Union from 1922 to 1952, during which time he killed far more people than Hitler ever managed. Now, with the collapse of the Soviet Union and an apparently "democratic" Russia, Vladimir Putin has become another political powerhouse there, and has much of the world shaking in their boots by running the country a bit like how the mafia would still like to run Chicago. He served as a KGB foreign intelligence officer for 16 years before retiring to politics. Maybe it's the cold and dreary weather that makes the leaders of Russia so grumpy. But it's difficult to know exactly what Putin is up to domestically and internationally. He is an example of a world leader who thrives on being an enigma so, if you want your path to power to involve other people putting you there rather than the support of the voting public, there is much to learn from how Putin is able to terrify the West while doing or saying very little. There are occasional attempts to question whether he is really as bad as he seems, but his history in foreign intelligence has most who look further into his morals dismissing such a notion. He sits on the throne because he has his opponents murdered or imprisoned, while ensuring that any domestic media attempts to question his methods are surveilled and intimidated into towing the line. Recently he has also started meddling in foreign elections which shows that, while a physical conquest of other nations is no longer a game world leaders play, that does not mean they do not look outward and seek to control it in other ways.

Money will be the most important form of influence to be obtained on your journey to becoming a world leader. Unless you take an enigmatic Putin route, it is likely that the second most valuable resource you can have is good public speaking. Adolf Hitler, perhaps the most loathed individual from history, was nevertheless extremely commanding and persuasive as a public speaker. Nazi Germany would probably never have happened if crowds of people weren't convinced into getting incensed by what he was telling them about the Motherland being under attack from everything foreign and different. He knew instinctively what content would rile people and get them to support him. So much so that the German people were soon ready to go to war with pretty much the whole world. That's some scary influence and Donald Trump's rise to power shows it is not the case that the lesson has been learned as to how persuasive an adept public speaker can be. Not to compare the two men in all respects – hopefully Trump isn't that bad (fingers crossed) – but the current President of the United States is hardly seen as a great intellect, and yet his public speaking alone proved enough to overcome every single media jibe about his hair and personality.

Staying on Hitler for a moment, because it might also be helpful to point out that a sense of identity and homeland is not even that important when seeking power, in that the spark which ignited German nationalism was not even German, but Austrian. It's like Donald Trump achieving what he has while being Canadian as well but, if people are hearing what they want to hear, they are happy to be hypocrites just as much as politicians and get right behind you.

As already mentioned, don't let being female put you off either. There are quite a few who have kicked up enough dirt around their skirt tails to earn a paragraph or two in the history books and the list is growing. Okay so Benazir Bhutto was assassinated, but if you're mad enough to run for power in Pakistan then you're probably looking to end up a martyr rather than sitting in a cozy retirement home with your feet up.

The female leader to have kicked up the biggest stink, however, was probably Margaret Thatcher. One of the most influential politicians in British history, she certainly didn't shy away from divisive policies. Indeed, her methods were so controversial that they earned the right of falling into their own category of political ideas, known as Thatcherism. Thatcher was the first female in history to hold the position of British Prime Minister. Her reign had its fair share of ups and downs and she even narrowly escaped an assassination attempt. She became known as the "Iron Lady" because, at the time, it was socially unacceptable for the Russian journalist who gave her the nickname to publicly call her a bitch. In the UK to this day there is no sitting on the fence regarding Thatcher. If you're right-wing you think she was the best thing to happen to the country; if you're left wing you think she was evil. Even a sensitive portrayal of her final years when she was suffering from dementia, which won Meryl Streep another Oscar, has failed to soften the stance of her critics.

If none of those do it for you then have a trawl through Wikipedia to find a method with which you can feel at home. Whether you want to be a power-crazed loon like Uganda's Idi Amin Dad, a nightmare in a shiny suit and polished forehead like Syria's Bashir al-Assad, or even pretend to be a fine, patriotic statesman like Winston Churchill. All of them played the game to get where they were and are. So, find a guru and become their apprentice – just never let on that who it is that your approach is based on.

Chapter 3: Personality Traits of a World Leader

If you want to be a world leader, then you probably already have the personality traits necessary to successfully sit upon the throne. You have to be a special level of arrogant if you want to have that much power. World leaders are extremely confident, which is commonly perceived as being arrogant or having a large ego. People may label you as being a narcissist. In fact, there are many famous world leaders all throughout history who have been described as being severely narcissistic. There is a fine line that must be toed during a political reign, and often it is misinterpreted as being self-centered. You have to act like a boss who knows how to get people to follow your orders. How else do you get a room full of other self-centered politicians to be a bunch of "yes men"? But, who cares what you get labeled?! You can't be too thin-skinned in this business. Critics and internet trolls will throw mud at you just for the sake of seeing if anything sticks. Having negativity as part of your career narrative is unavoidable in politics. The trick is to position yourself in a way that it doesn't hurt you. For all his misogyny and ignorance, Donald Trump has not presented himself as a shining example of moral virtue. He has presented himself as a successful businessman and, in this respect, the media cannot lay a glove on him. Stories about grabbing women 'by the pussy' do his reputation little harm, because it was never that righteous anyway. Whereas his predecessor, President Obama, would probably have never recovered from such a revelation, just as President Clinton never really did from being a naughty boy who tells fibs.

Charm is a useful personality trait, more so in today's digital age than it has ever been throughout history. Even so, charm comes in many guises and it is important to think of whatever charm you choose as a performance, rather than as a window into your soul. It might sound like a contradiction in terms but, in many respects, charm can also be thought of as deception. A homeless bum who walks into a crowded room, announcing himself at great volume and remarking on how beautiful the women look tonight will not come across as particularly charming – but get him showered, stick a designer Brioni on him and make him a billionaire, then suddenly all the ladies swoon.

Learn where your own charm/deception fits, so it can be applied to whatever situation you find yourself in. If you don't have the wallet or the accent to pull off looking like you belong beside the pool of a luxury yacht then don't worry. A working-class twang can be endearing coming from someone who appears to have bettered themselves, crawling out of the mud clean-faced and looking as if dirt has never stained them. Contrary to what many presume, numerous individuals have made a name for themselves from lowly, even desperate positions. Billionaires Howard Schultz, Harold Simmons and Ralph Lauren, for example, while actors Sylvester Stallone, Jennifer Lopez, Halle Berry and Daniel Craig all flirted with homelessness. Okay so none of these are currently world leaders, but are you telling me that Daniel Craig couldn't become prime minister of the UK if he really put his mind to it? Certainly, against the current competition it hardly seems like the task would be much of a struggle. We're not exactly in an era of political heavyweights.

Once your ability to perform and charm yourself in any given situation has been honed to perfection, with contacts to boot, then you have a sound base for a springboard into power. At that point, as long as you don't waver or crumble under the public gaze, the rest of it becomes relatively easy. In a world of overexposure, a highly-resourced marketing team will easily make the most of your appeal and all that is left is for the camera to capture your charm and then distribute it to people all over the world with the swipe of a finger. The masses will warm to a turd with glitter on if presented to them in the right context.

All your hard work should go into the preparation, as if you've written the script and designed the storyboards for this play yourself and are only preparing to see it play out as envisioned. The factors the camera won't see and the people who vote for you will never know about. The bargaining, the negotiating and the alliance forming are the real tools that will turn you into a world leader. Rich and important people will still decide, even if they can't predict the electorate at the moment. They are the ones that will place you in the starting blocks for that race to power.

If you are not naturally extroverted then now is the time to practice. Think of every meeting and situation as a performance and you will soon be aspiring to a level of fakery that makes a successful politician. Introverted people will not pull this off, unless you can at least outwardly change your nature. Don't trust the people to see the good in you just because you think that, deep down, you have a heart of gold. They won't. If you do not naturally come across as charismatic and relatable then learn to act in a way that achieves this in spite of your true self.

You need to find a way to be loud and proud; to thrive on crowds and controversy, rather than shrinking from anything challenging. Consider how popular some actors are. That is because people fall in love with a performance, not with a person. Like with any good quality relationship, the people want to be courted and wooed first, then they will accept your proposal, before being fucked.

Chapter 4: Training and Skills Required

Education

It was previously believed that you must have a pristine education in economic law or political science for a renowned Ivy League school, in order to have the perquisites of a world leader. The 2016 U.S. election, however, has debunked that myth. We would like to think that the person whom we elect as the one to develop policies, to represent us in our global economy and to hold the key to the nuclear codes, would at the very least know how to appropriately wear the comb-over on a windy day. We now know that anyone can become a world leader. This, however controversial, opens up exciting possibilities.

It helps if you have some form of educational background. Even if it's a meager liberal arts degree from a local community college. You graduated, and that shows that you can complete something. Bravo, you are almost ready.

Make sure you know how to use Twitter. It is not the same as Facebook or Instagram. Your number of Twitter followers directly translates into how relevant of a political candidate you are. If you enter into a presidential campaign with a pathetic 1,000 followers, then just bend over and give in to those who took the time to gain a healthy following of almost one million before bothering to sign up for the race.

Currently it seems that your use of Twitter, for all topics of interest, will be your most valuable tool. It used to be the news headlines that were everything, but now you can afford them to be negative so long as you have a shouting, brainless bunch of internet trolls who cry elitist conspiracy every time someone criticizes you. They're like soldier ants clearing out the hive with maximum efficiency, even though there is ultimately nothing in it for them. All you need is a filter for the mind control, meaning that the first person you need to hire is a social media/PR expert. They must follow you everywhere you go and advise on your every move, down to the most trivial tweet. This way, you will know when it is appropriate to be witty, or what global and/or domestic issues deserve serious comments. If they are worth their salt they can advise you when and in what manner to act shocked because some atrocious event has occurred, when to get on your high-horse because someone else in the public eye has dropped a testicle, and when to stay away from murky water, even though you do actually feel the need to comment on the latest celebrity nipple slip or revenge porn.

Don't worry though, as there will be occasions on which you can have fun with social media too. Indeed, sometimes one of the best things you can do is to be controversial. On this score, as much as I might hate to admit it, Donald Trump has to be named as the master, even to the point of blending his controversy with another modern political phenomenon of fake news. For example, in 2015 he tweeted 'The United Kingdom is trying hard to disguise their massive Muslim problem. Everybody is wise to what is happening, very sad! Be honest.' In the minutes and hours following this gem, the fact that tweeters across the Atlantic were going to town on how monumentally stupid this claim was did nothing to harm Trump's ability to fuel the anti-Muslim vote in the US. Indeed, the more criticism he received for such claims the more he was able to claim that he was being unfairly treated by a prejudiced liberal media.

It will help to have a strategic approach to whatever chaos and turmoil your nation is currently feeling. The question is not who do you upset, but rather what picture is painted of you as a result of those people being upset? And what picture is painted of you by those who jump to your defense, or even remain in silent agreement appreciating the fact that you are willing to talk sense and speak up about what some do not respect or want to hear.

Public Speaking

As mentioned before, you will need to develop high quality, distinguished, public speaking skills. You don't necessarily need to say anything of importance when you speak. You simply need to have a few words that will make people stand, clap, and wave a flag or sign. The way you say it is what really matters. Some great words to include are, together, win, great, fight, change, better, workers, nation and freedom. Just repeat those words, as crowds respond to positivity even if there's nothing robust about your manifesto. Glue them together by filler words in different ways, and you'll be right as rain. If you hate writing speeches, hire someone. No need to fact-check the speech beforehand. The people don't care if what you say is true. Just as long as you hit them in the feels and say things like, "All my life I have fought for freedom and I will continue to fight. I publicly opposed that bill, and together we will change what has been done to the hard workers of this great nation, and fight for better freedom." See how easy it is to say what people want to hear, without really saying anything at all? Easy peasy.

Don't be too sensitive about shying away from humor or mockery either. A certain Mr Churchill might advise you that an annoying vocal inflection is an asset, while easy to replicate mannerisms serve to imbed your persona into the public consciousness. You certainly don't want to look and sound like everyone else. If God ever bothered to design the perfect politician then the public would probably be too stupid to elect them. Instead they'd elect the idiot standing next to him pulling wacky faces and tripping up the steps on the way to shake his opponent's hand, all because he makes them smile a bit more.

Remember, it's charm over substance every time. Learn to sit back and enjoy it if people decide to mock you, because if they do this they are really exposing a growing obsession for you. People don't want to idolize you like how they might a rock star. Your job could not be much more uncool, but they are quite capable of voting for someone they can also make fun of. The impressionists who will take you on will have no material if you're not famous enough to make jokes about, so don't think of comedians as obstacles either. They're puppies following you around, looking up to you and wishing they were you. When they successfully exploit any vulnerable characteristics you have, that only makes you look more human anyway. Take it in

your stride and laugh so that people see you don't take yourself too seriously – even if this isn't true and deep down you're becoming more neurotic with every sting. As you make your mark, you'll even learn about giving them easy content to use and you should absolutely maximize this.
Certainly, don't look at the media as a problem just because some of them are too left or right wing for your tastes. Regardless of where they appear to stand, all they actually want is content to fill their pages and broadcasts with. You will be in a privileged position of deciding in what manner that content plays out. Play them like a middle man who doesn't know whether he's coming or going. If you sense a bad headline coming from somewhere, throw them a curve ball and they'll run with that instead, trying to figure out what it all means even if it doesn't mean anything.

Appearance

Spend some time in front of a mirror and practice your smile and wave technique. It's important that you appear inviting. You don't want your smile to say "I'm crazy", or your wave to say, "I watch too much 'I Love Lucy'". Maybe point a finger and bring your hands together every once in a while, then give a slight bow of gratitude. Appearing gracious after you finish a speech makes the people feel like they are doing a good thing by supporting you, and that you are thankful for their support and contributions.

Key to any world leader's success, is their ability to bargain. If you can't dish out your bargaining chips appropriately then you're wasting your time. Come to the table with a lot of ammunition, ready to fire offers and counter offers to political lobbyists who threaten to back the other candidate or to release the private details of your history of drug abuse. You will need to do your research ahead of time. Know who will be there and what they are most likely to ask for. Think of it as a game of poker. Just as they claim to have info about a crazy weekend trip to Cabo when you were 25, if you've done your homework, then you can claim to know information that could potentially be just as harmful if it were to become public knowledge. A great way to remove any opportunity for blackmail is to disclose all past and present shortcomings as soon as you hit the political stage. Maybe write a book titled, "My life, my mistakes, and all of the things I need to say in order to gain your vote."

If you are born into money or happen upon a small fortune, and find that there is a skill that you would benefit from along the campaign trail, then hire someone to either teach it to you or to make it easy for you to pretend that you know it.

Fake it until you make it. For example, if you claim to be excellent at baking and you invite a potentially large donor to your home, you need to either learn how to bake as well as you claim or pay someone to do it for you.

Somewhere along the road, all world leaders must debate an opponent. This may possibly be one of the most important skills to have, but the most difficult to obtain. It helps if you can bribe the moderators into letting you know which questions are going to be asked. If for some reason you can't do that, then you'll need to do a substantial amount of homework to find out what the hot topics are and what your opponents will likely give as answers and rebuttals. You're better off honing in your bargaining skills in an effort to avoid playing the painful game of guess the question.

Chapter 5: Dress for Success – face value

It goes without saying, you have to look the part if you are going to be a world leader. In that position you are a public figure so, by default, you are a brand ambassador. Anything you wear must be carefully considered and gain a royal stamp of approval. This might sound stressful if you're not particularly fashion savvy, but you won't be lacking in choice and will soon start to develop a persona based on costume. Once you have the big money behind your campaign, designers will be throwing clothes at you and your spouse also, so you will be able to choose from the best.

Former President of the United States, Barack Obama, and his wife Michelle Obama were two of the best dressed people of their time. Occasionally, you could catch Barack strolling around outside in machine-washed Dad jeans. Michelle was seen wearing a tank top and mom shorts while helping children plant a garden. She looked like someone straight off the cover of Home and Garden Magazine. They were a picturesque couple, and it was comforting to see them in clothing that was not always prim and proper.

There is a time and place for your favorite jeans, however. When there is a need for you to address the nation, then there probably is also a need to put on your fancy pants. No worries though. There will be someone there telling you what to wear every step of the way. Your clothes will be so perfect that they'll match the weather, complement the wallpaper and even your daughter's party dress.

Women have a more difficult challenge in finding the perfect wardrobe to wear, as society is still less forgiving to the female form. No matter how you go about it, there will be some wife-beating man and caddy make-up caked female news anchor waiting around every corner to talk about your overly conservative power suit or your frumpy-assed mom shorts. You can't blame them though. They have been raised in a world that naturally does that to women. It helps to look at them as victims. They are merely a product of their environment (and employer), trying to survive in an uneducated world that only relates to tangible, simple thoughts. It is likely there will be some soldiering on through lose-lose situations, as you're never going to draw the eye like a supermodel – even if you have the body it would be inappropriate to do so. You will have to somehow look like you're attending a job interview every time you step out of the door, but without ever really doing sexy. Too much leg or cleavage and you're in the wrong newspaper columns. But try to look too much like a businessman and they'll start using the word androgyny every time they talk about you – and not in a good way.

That phrase about not 'judging a book by its cover' is an ironic one in that everyone involved with marketing books knows that readers do just that. It's the same with politics. Do you seriously think they're going to get to page 16 of your manifesto and declare 'This is superb, I'm voting for this one'? Of course not. They are going to be watching your performance and, if they spend any time wondering 'Why are they wearing that?' then the performance will be missed. So, your outfit has to impress in a way that isn't at all distracting. If so, game over. Unless, of course, you are trying to distract people from the words that come out of your mouth. That's a completely different tactic, if you want them to decide to elect 'the character'. Donald Trump has achieved this, not with his clothes, but with his ridiculous hair. The UK has a similar thing going on with a clown by the name of Boris Johnson who might well be running for prime minister himself very soon. If so then unruly blond hair will soon be seen as a stereotypical sign of political power.

Chapter 6: Getting the Vote and Policies for Winners

You will need to pick a side. If you want to sit on the throne, you have to speak about the policies that people are concerned with, and you have to tell them exactly what they want to hear. If you're trying to gain the votes of people who tend to be more conservative, then you don't support abortion and you own a bunch of guns. If you're attempting to win the hearts of liberals, then smoke some weed and say you will reverse the effects of climate change. It really is as simple as that. You can talk to people on both sides of the argument and ask them why they always vote for that side. Many of them will scratch their heads and say, "I don't know, that's just how I've always done it."

You may also think that gaining the support of celebrities holds a lot of merit, so go with policies that they care about. Well, up until this past year, I would have agreed with that thought. However, most of the entertainment world publicly opposed Donald Trump. Their efforts to stop him proved to be futile, so it can be a desperate move to align yourself with people who are genuinely popular unless you really know what you're doing.

Choosing policies to stand behind will automatically put you into a political party. Some places, like France for example, do not put two large parties above the others. Their most recent election was won by a President that ran independent of their two main parties. Their candidates could toe the line on some of the topics, or could choose not to care about a particular topic. In large countries like the U.S., if you are not running as a Democrat (liberal) or Republican (conservative), then you don't stand a chance. In this situation, you can't toe the line of both sides. You have to be one or the other on all topics if you want to have a chance at the throne. The U.S. has even gone so far as to stupefy its election process. Voters can click an "easy" button at the top of the screen that will choose either all republican candidates or all democratic candidates. There's no need to do any research about the candidates who are running. They could be voting for an ex-sex offender, as long as their policies are conservative, then they are okay to be in charge of a country.

It's easy to get caught up in the effects of bargaining, black mail, and life changing events that change your stance on policies. As you begin to seek out financial support for your campaign, you will be asked to support certain policies in order to get help. Also, maybe you had a death in the family that made you reevaluate your stance on gun control. You want to avoid flip-flopping as much as possible. Changing your stance on political hot topics halfway through a campaign can be detrimental to all of your hard work. Remember, right now you have to pick a side. Once you have won, then you can go back on your word and not do all of the things that you promised. This is the legacy of most presidents. Don't forget to consider reelection though. As long as you do one or two large things that you promised during your campaign, then you will most likely find yourself on the throne to serve a second term.

Whatever your approach, remember the sheep in a field analogy. It is all about where the voters are standing and sometimes even an apparent contradiction can increase your flock. For example, so long as one of your opponents doesn't already control the narrative on a particular issue, it is entirely possible to steal some of their core support, especially if they remain on a high-horse about adopting a particular policy. A good example is when left-wing politicians succeed in stealing right-wing voters by promising to be hard on immigration. This is often a sensitive topic, so candidates make the mistake about not talking about it. As a left-wing politician, you have the comfort zone of knowing that your core support sees right-wing parties as hating foreigners and so, even if you alarm some of them, you will not lose them on this issue to an opponent they despise. In comparison, if you are right-wing, a good cause on which you can steal votes from the left is by appearing to embrace green energy and being concerned about climate change. The last prime minister of the UK, the conservative David Cameron, adopted this tactic by cycling into Parliament every day when opposition leader, while also drawing the homosexual vote by bringing in gay marriage – much to the distaste of his own mother.

Chapter 7: Creating Alliances

You're going to need friends in high places if you plan to reign for any significant amount of time. Get used to the fact that, as the most powerful person in the world, you may also become the most hated person – whether fairly or unfairly. By default, that puts a giant target on your head. In order to protect yourself, you're going to need allies and henchman. Both the seen and the unseen gang of minions who back you up, firefight media disasters, divide your opponents and outwit potential power grabbers from inside your own party. At every level, whether at home or on the international stage, in the media or in the business community, everyone must fear your ability to retaliate against them on some level.

Foreign policy is one avenue of government that showcases this necessity more than any other. Different countries are never really friends or allies on a political level. All your counterparts overseas are interested in is money, not history or heritage, regardless of what wars you once fought in together. If interests can be aligned, you will speak fondly of your two nations' histories as an unbreakable bond. If you are opponents on the world stage then it doesn't matter how many lives were saved by working together. It's all about where the money is flowing, which is precisely why the West acts like a big best buddy to Saudi Arabia, where husbands have their wives stoned if they happen to look at another man. Saudi Arabia has a lot of oil, of course. If not, they would probably be shunned internationally and in a similar state of turmoil as other Middle East nations; Iraq, Iran, Syria, etc.

Come baring gifts to establish robust trade agreements that will keep the world of trade and commerce a settled place during your time in office. Don't get excited by the idea of new economic structures. That will only lead to turmoil, so put up with capitalism and just make sure that your allies overseas are happy. Do some research into other foreign leaders' likes and dislikes. Starting a new foreign trade relationship is like moving into a new house. You never know what kind of neighbors you're going to get so be sure you bring them a jell-o mold or fresh baked cookies to set things off on the right foot. The last thing you want is for them to offer you a gift and for you to only have a piece of linty gum in your pocket, to offer in return. If they like to play golf, provide them with a top-of-the-line set of new clubs, signed by their favorite golf player.

Now that they like you because of your gift, you can play some bargaining chips. They will want your alliance just as much as you want theirs. However, it has to make sense for both leaders to enter into the agreement. Promise things like front row tickets to basketball games or UFC fights. Or, promise to transfer $2 million to an offshore account every year. Whatever kind of kickbacks you two agree on, let it be classified as Top Secret, and have that legal interpreter that you hired draft up some low level trade agreement for the public to believe was the result of the meeting. Allow the press to take pictures of both leaders signing the fake agreement and then go out to dinner and drinks to celebrate your new friendship.

Creating alliances is what will make or break a leader. You don't want a negotiation to end badly. The next thing you know, nobody will side with you and you'll be left playing all by yourself. So, come with money and trinkets enough to guarantee that you leave with allies.

Chapter 8: Creating Enemies

As I said in the previous chapter, you will create enemies on your journey. It's the nature of the beast. But there is no need to fear these enemies so long as you have chosen them wisely. You could probably do something to help a small nation like Venezuela at the moment, but doing so would only send out a mixed message. Much better to keep them in your bad books for electing someone with the audacity to speak out against other world leaders (the delightfully bonkers Nicolas Maduro who spends his time having conference calls with celebrity criminals trapped in overseas embassies, rather than trying to reverse the economic depression he has caused by rejecting capitalism).

Perhaps the most complicated aspect of all this is the enemies you may inherit. If your predecessors have made bad calls they tend to stick around and sometimes it's all about managing the problem rather than fixing. The obvious example of such a problem managed rather than answered is with the rivalry between Israel and Palestine. The West might have concocted this situation many years ago – as it did with Yugoslavia for those of you who remember that – but fixing it is just not on the agenda. Might make us all look bad. So, managing the problem by staging sensitive and 'productive' peace talks will remain the approach until the day when one side of the equation is accidentally wiped out in a war. Hence, it will fix itself.

This is kind of also the policy with North Korea – in that waging a war against them will just be too expensive. Although there is the risk of them nuking us all at some point. So that one is a tense situation. Do you have the nerve to keep an itchy trigger finger off your own nukes? Or should we just go for it seeing as we've a bigger arsenal at our disposal? Most likely some smart diplomat will advise you when matters have really gone that far, so don't worry about needing to have the powers of perception to outwit Kim Jong-un. Just as it's impossible to talk sense to a fool, it's impossible to outwit someone who doesn't have any wits.

Chapter 9: Money Money Money

Mentioned in almost every chapter, so I think it's necessary to dedicate an entire chapter to the topic. You must have money. If you have enough money, nothing can stop you. If there is one universal language, the one thing that everybody wants, it's power. And money is power – hence, everything.

You're lucky if you're born into money. You'll be taught at a young age how to take advantage of your wealth, how to persuade and how to make valuable purchases. If you never have to worry about money, then you are left with plenty of time to worry about things that really matter. You can hire people to do your household chores, which will leave you with even more time to dedicate to the important things. Vacations, socializing, collectable cars, drinking and procreating. That's what we were really put on this earth to do. To enjoy life's many pleasures. If you're always concerned with not having enough money, then you're merely surviving.

As the heir to a fortune, your opinions automatically hold more merit than those struggling to manage their debts. Lower class citizens ignorantly associate wealth with knowledge. So use that to your advantage when you begin your journey as a world leader. Your power of persuasion extends beyond the depths of your pockets. You have people who want your friendship. They will support anything you or your family has to say or any of your endeavors, no matter how big or small. You don't need to put in the time to build a valuable network. Many people spend years developing a network of five or six valuable acquaintances. You'll have hundreds of valuable people at your disposal all the time.

You're negotiating power is also stronger being a person born with money. You have spent your life negotiating and bargaining. You know all too well how to use your money to get what you want. Buy a hooker or two for the old congressman whose wife has dementia and promise him a spot as secretary of defense, as long as he will vote for your new healthcare bill. Give a judge courtside season tickets to every LA Laker's game if he agrees to rule your new immigration bill as constitutional.

If you're not born with money, then you're starting off under unfortunate circumstances. That means you have to marry into it, inherit it, or work for it. All of those options suck. If you marry into it, then you are only entitled to a small portion of it if you get divorced. If you inherit a fortune, that means someone had to die. If you have to work for it, then just don't even bother. Without a job that pays millions, then you'll be wasting your time flipping burgers.

If you aren't born to money then you'll also need to learn how to appropriately use it once you finally get what you need. Bargaining won't come natural to you and negotiations will be intimidating. Not perfecting these skills will hinder your efforts just as much as not having any money to bargain with.

Chapter 10: More Power

More money, more power. The more money you continue to get, the more power you will gain. Bribery is the name of the game. Getting people to do what you want is what politics are all about and everybody has a price. No matter their personal values, or what kind of campaign they ran before, everybody has an amount they will switch teams for. Maybe they have grandchildren who are in serious college debt. Maybe they want to buy a second home in the Bahamas. You don't care what the reason is, all you care about is that you have enough money to give you the power to buy their support.

The more money you have, the more information you have on your opponents as well. Maybe you are having difficulties persuading a particular individual and need another form of leverage. So pay for someone to dig up some nasty skeleton buried deep in the closet and blackmail them into doing what you want. The corridors of power are constructed with such webs of deceit and, if you find this tasteless, you can be sure that all of your adversaries, even those in your own party, are looking to do exactly the same so that they can have leverage with you.

In the global economy, more money equates to more purchasing power. In terms of campaigning, it serves to make political ideologies and the contest of left versus right obsolete. Evening the playing field. Whichever side you approach from, remember that you are building a construct and the values and principles incorporated into that construct in order to win votes are decoration only. Regardless of what you claim to stand by, once in office there is always a reason for going against type and raising taxes if you need to. Blame the economy and world events, then have yourself portrayed in the media as someone willing to take the tough decisions even when you found them tasteless. The markets will thank you for it while the general populace go back to whining about politicians as they always have. This scenario is unavoidable; the lower classes will ultimately hate you – unless you do your job poorly, end up getting assassinated and become a martyr. Choose which outcome you prefer: a retirement of being invited to glamorous behind-closed-door parties fueled with cocaine and loose women, or a cold grave while your opponents swoop in and steal the limelight.

Chapter 11: This Means War

You'll be at war as soon as you begin your fight to the top until the second someone else is sworn into office. You'll be at war with your opponents in the beginning. They'll do everything in their power to crush your campaign and keep you from reaching your full potential. Through sabotage, blackmail, or simply having more money, you will be on the frontline of the political battlefield as you run to become a world leader.

Don't kid yourself though. Once you're elected, the resistance doesn't end. Those who were rooting for the other guy, will attempt to block your every move. A silent game of chess will begin, forcing you to move back and forth with negotiations while sidestepping any and all efforts to make you crumble under the pressure. Haven't you seen how the incredibly successful Game of Thrones is advertised? "When you play the game of thrones you win or you die." This remains as true today as it did back in medieval fantasy land. The game never sits still and you must always be the one with the biggest appetite, or else it is you that will be eaten.

Try to run a country that is busy. Keep as many of the citizens occupied as you can and, with those you can't, ensure that the media content they receive does not play to any of the narratives your opponents would like to see unite them. They can be discontented, as long as they are discontented in a useless way that makes them look naïve. Remember, as leader, it is you who controls the media narrative by deciding what political content to put out there. Takeover only becomes possible when your approach is exhausted, but shouldn't be allowed to happen purely through your opponent's cunning. This is what happened when President George Bush Sr. failed to see Bill Clinton coming in 1993. He thought he was strong and stable enough in his position to not need to take Clinton on but, in effect, he handed Clinton the electoral narrative by not being the one applying himself to the façade of media focus.

As well as war with domestic opponents, you may also face the issue of actually fighting a war against another country. If so then the earlier work made forming alliances will pay off and, in the event that someone declares war on you, the matter can actually be dealt with very simply. They are the aggressor so almost any manner of retaliation – excepting anything classed as war crimes – is not going to upset your own supporters, who you can claim to be protecting by bombing citizens in distant lands.

Should you decide to wage your own war, however, then things become murkier and you will need to be certain about what you want to achieve in advance. Recent military operations in Iraq and Afghanistan have turned peoples against their leaders for dragging on with no real aim, accompanied by more unpredictable regions as a result. Somehow the US failed to learn from Vietnam in this respect, although this was caused by something of a perfect storm, being a response to September 11th at a time when a guy who was quite keen on a bit of war – George Bush Jr – was in the White House. You may very well be compelled to act in some way, but if so make sure you either have an endgame or a get-out. President Obama – thought by many to be one of the more peaceful presidents – was actually fairly cunning in this respect regarding Libya. He maintained an impression of being half-hearted about the military intervention, allowed Britain and France to lead the way, while making sure there was at least a feasible endgame with the removing of dictator Colonel Gadaffi. This was achieved but, even though he has called this 'the worst mistake' of his Presidency, what he has really done has found a way to appear humble about the intervention, rather than as a villain. Consequently, he receives far less stick about Libya than his predecessor does about Iraq, as

Bush remains in a position of trying to make out the war was a positive development.

Chapter 12: Brainwash and Serve Another Term

So, you've pulled off a period in power, made your way into the history books and now a cushy retirement awaits. Why would you prolong your stay? Get out while matters are still good and you can claim a bit of a 'legacy' just to annoy your critics, then watch some amateur come along and fall flat on their face because of the mess you've been covering up that is now left behind for them.

That said, power is addictive. There are those who can simply not give up the status and, as it turns out, if you plan on being one of these imbeciles there might yet be many years in office awaiting you. Recent times show numerous examples of nations having elected frauds, philanderers and nitwits who have presented their case for re-election and successfully remained in place.

Many people asked themselves the question of how did George Bush Jr. possibly gain a second term in office. He came across as a buffoon, never knowing which door to open to get out of a press conference and caught playing golf whenever his people were suffering some kind of natural disaster. Yet, he never really looked like being kicked out. Nevertheless, he is just the tip of the iceberg on this score. Re-elections that leave voters scratching their heads happen all the time. Bush's war buddy Tony Blair was also reelected after the invasion of Iraq, even though his reputation never really recovered from pretending Saddam Hussein had weapons of mass destruction. It remains the consensus in the UK, even within his own party, that he lied – 'but we'll still vote you in for a third term' said the electorate. France also allowed President Jacques Chirac to spend 12 years in office before this shady character ended up being convicted of fraud in 2011. Well done with that one. But the biggest biscuit has to have been taken by Italy's Silvio Berlusconi. This is a man who appeared to use his position of prime minster to bed as many prostitutes as possible and who once called Germany's Chancellor, Angela Merkel, an 'unfuckable lard bucket'. Something of a diplomatic embarrassment, but no less than four reelections surely proves that Italians have a great sense of humor.

Remarkably, all these loathsome individuals were able to keep the media on their side. It is as if, once an allegiance has been gained, journalists start sticking up for a particular politician and stick with it because they are too proud to admit when they are wrong about someone. The truth is that the media are very easy to manipulate, especially they are now obsessed with 24-hour output. They will rush and stampede to report on issues before they even know if it's worth the effort, so long as the right carrot is dangled. I could call my local media source right now, claim there is a hostage situation on the corner of 4th street and Park Avenue and there would be 4 to 6 news vans showing up at that location only to find that there is, in fact, nothing to report on. There could be a backpack left on a bench somewhere and all we need is for some moron to say, "It could be a bomb". Suddenly 12 news vans and floods of reporters are on the scene, reporting for hours as the bomb squad carefully reveals that it's only a bag full of dirty gym clothes. The overreaction of our media is ridiculous but in the matter of persuading the masses to vote for you in for a second term, it's quite advantageous.

The overstimulation and overexposure that we get through the news and social media leaves people confused and, oftentimes, emotionally charged every time they turn on the TV or look at their phone. Use this to your advantage to brainwash viewers into electing you to serve a second term. Leak false information that will put citizens into a tizzy and then air a public statement geared at making people feel safe and secure under your protection.

It helps when the media is encouraged to make your enemies the public's enemies as well. If the nation feels threatened by a foreign leader and believes that you are successfully using the power of love to keep the peace, they can now rest easy under the false security that you will do what is best for them and their families.

Another great way to get those news anchors to waste their time is to slowly throw your opponent under the bus. Don't forget, Putin used social media to sabotage the 2016 U.S. election. He was able to get the citizens of the U.S. to revisit the argument that a presidential candidate had used her personal internet server to send classified emails. Woah! How rebellious of her?! One candidate was being accused of sexual assault and sued for fraud, while the other one sent a few emails from her bathroom. Which one did the media tell us to be up in arms about? The lady who works and poops at the same time. We may never know exactly how much interference there was in that election, but it's a great way to demonstrate how useful the media is in persuading viewers.

You may find that your approval ratings need improvement if you are to be reelected. If so, lie about it. Get someone to report on a false poll that shows your approval rating up among that of legends. Did a small crowd show up for your national address? That's what Photoshop is for. Make it look better than it was, and history will know no different. Don't concern yourself with the truth. Only concern yourself with the fact that the public are waiting to be convinced. Blame all the bad things that are being said about you on your opponents, cry media conspiracy and the unhappy beggars will put their X in that box yet again. Just like the media, they don't like to admit they were wrong either and that the kindhearted souls elected a bastard.

One surefire way to improve your chances of reelection is to use the media to make people feel like there was a serious threat to national security, and that you alone were the one who stopped it. Obama isn't the one who killed Bin Laden, but he sure did take more credit than the Navy Seal who pulled the trigger. Even more convenient, Bin Laden was killed on May 2, 2011; right as Obama was going to be campaigning for a second term. Coincidence? Call me cynical if you like.

Chapter 13: The Truth About Western World Leaders

There are more he-said she-said rumors floating around the internet then there are blood cells in the human body. Many believe that this massive amount of rumors is meant to be white noise so that people can't focus on or believe the ones that are true. The really diligent minions who get their rocks off by following everything to do with politics, take the time to check sources and dig really deep into the validity of conspiracy theories, and how they originated. Some truths are claimed conspiracy theories, because it's better that the truth is not known.

Another very wise thing Hitler once said was, "How fortunate for governments that the people they administer do not think." It's a tough pill to swallow, but Hitler was on to something. Conspiracy theories gain merit because of stupid people. The more stupid people there are, the more the conspiracy theory grows and is validated. Now we are left with the difficult task of weeding out truths from lies, to figure out who is really in charge, and what (if anything) can we do about it.

If you live your life looking on the bright side, one great thing that has come from Trump's reign is his blatant disregard for covering up shady deals. He puts little time and effort into attempting to make his voters think that he has their best interests at heart. From the people he appoints to run government programs, to his frequent trips to fancy golf courses, it's become pretty obvious that the only language the president speaks is money. He puts the CEO of an oil empire in charge of the EPA, a known right-wing extremist as head of national security, and a woman set on bringing down public education in charge of the Department of Education. The common denominator is money. Large corporations benefit from putting one of their puppets into the game. Now, they call the shots, they write the bills and they get more money. Now, if we try to think rationally about this, it doesn't have to be a bad thing. If big businesses have more money, doesn't that mean they should be able to employ more people or pay their employees higher wages? In theory, yes. In reality, stop entertaining the idea, because it will never happen.

Oil, insurance and pharmaceuticals are the puppeteers who run the show, and apparently also Russia. They are the ones paying for their puppets to fill the chairs of department heads. This comes as no surprise, being business as usual. For example, why did wearing your seatbelt become a law? Because insurance companies don't want to pay medical bills for the idiots who don't wear their seatbelts. Why do windmills get off the wall reasons for being voted down? "They kill the birds" "They're an eye sore". Because big oil and coal typhoons watch their businesses literally burn out if everyone supports renewable energy.

Where we come to a standstill on all conspiracy theories is when state representatives get in a room and try to agree on something. It's quite comical to see these people argue like schoolkids in the cafeteria. They are just as confused about the truth as the rest of us poor peasants. The only difference is that we, the peasants, actually voted those children into their position. I'm sure there was money involved in their political journey as well, but not like the money required by the person running for president. The fear that motivates state representatives is not being voted in for another term. If they don't post a selfie on the internet of themselves fighting for the people, then they will lose if they run again. All they need to do is make the people of the state that they represent believe that they are fighting for better education, lower taxes, and lower unemployment, and they can sleep well at night knowing that they will most likely see another term. This process gives the people false hope that they are still in control of the country.

Chapter 14: Summary/Conclusion

We like to think that politics has come a long way since the days of trading pigs for land. However, we now know that persuasive power is still the key factor in our political realm. If you want to make it to the top, you have to come equipped with pockets full of bargaining chips. You won't get far without money, and a good sense of when and where to put it.

Whether you want to be president of the U.S., or reign terror on your kingdom like Vladimir Putin, you will need money and a whole bunch of good words. You'll need to be relentless in your actions. Narcissism should come natural to the psycho who wants to be in charge of this mess, and should find it easy to tune out cries for empathy.

Females who want to rule will need a rich husband and a pocket full of Pamperin. She will need to be ten times more persuasive than her male counterparts and she will need to leave her heartstrings at the door. Within the walls of political debate rooms, there is no room for empathy. Whether she has good or bad intentions, she needs to be louder and prouder than any man in the room. The gentle sex she is not.

There are simple actions you can take to convince the people that you are going to do what is best for them. The media is your best tool, so use it to your advantage. What you say does not need to be fact. It helps though, if your words hit people in the feel goods. They will act on emotions more than truths, so that is where you want to aim. Take some selfies while shaking hands with the leader of a homeless shelter. Allow the paparazzi to "accidentally" find out that you're down at the VA Hospital, making a large donation to help rebuild their facility. During the next Paris terrorist attack, flood your Twitter feed with condolences and words of unity and peace. This should get a good amount of people to rally behind you. It will help you to gain traction on the campaign trail, and will boost your approval ratings once you've taken over power.

You will need to look the part, all the time. Dress for the occasion, but always wear something that is the most powerful outfit in the room. If you're playing golf, wear the best golf gear. If you're exercising, sport the best shorts that UnderArmor has to offer. Make sure that all of your suits are steamed, tailored, and lay perfectly on your body. Remember to give Saturday Night Live something to pick on. Whether it be your hair, your tie, or the way you move your hands when you talk. You

need to take the comedic roasting like a champ
and laugh with the people.

Whether your do or don't agree with all of the
views on the left or right, unless you're in France
and can wink your way into office, you will have
to pick a side. In choosing a side you are, by
default, picking the people that you will need to
convince to vote for you. The easiest thing to do
is to look at which side has a historically better
voter turnout. This way, you know that your
chances to get more votes are higher simply by
default, even if your political interests lie more
closely with a party who has less support.

At the end of the day, make sure you come to the
playing field with buckets of money. More money,
more power. It doesn't matter how you get it. You
can be born with it, inherit it, marry into it, or
somehow work for it. Just make sure you come
knowing how to turn it into bargaining power.
Wheel and deal the days away until you have the
support you need to win the throne. Then,
continue using your money to form alliances with
other countries, and to keep your enemies
struggling to make any significant move against
you.

Finally, be sure to use the media to your
advantage. If there is a story that you don't want
people to pay attention to, make something up

that is more gossip worthy, and let the people argue over its validity, while the real ugly truths go unnoticed. Use the media to give the impression that you have good approval ratings. Also, be sure to time a significant event that makes you the hero, right as you begin campaigning for a second term. You're not a legitimate world leader, until you throw down your opponents and win the throne, twice.

Follow these simple steps, and get a lot of money, and you're soon to be sitting in one of the most powerful seats in the world.

Thank you for reading my book.

I would love it if you could leave me an honest review on what you thought of this book.

If you like to know more about my books and the opportunity to be notified of free promotions please visit www.Arylapublishing.com

Or follow @arylapublishing

 Facebook , Twitter and Instagram

Thank you

Preview Publications

How to Get a Rich Woman – By Tyler Moses (Comedy)

Are you a man who is ready to find yourself a sugar momma? Are you tired of conforming to traditional "bread-winner" expectations? Does your 9-5 factory job take too much time away from working towards your dream of becoming a Cross-fit champion, or professional video game reviewer? As society continues to progress, it is becoming even more clear that women should be the ones to bring home the bacon. Whether an unfortunate death left her with millions or she clawed her way up to the peak of Mt. Richmore, landing yourself a wealthy woman is the best way for you to reach your goals.

It is no secret that women love power. Allowing yourself to be the beta, giving her all of the alpha power, means that everyone gets what they want. She wants to be in charge and the one who successfully conquers all traditional male roles of power and influence. You get to reap the benefits of her success. Win-win. You could not ask for a more mutually beneficial relationship.

Out Now

How to Make Money Online –
By Fiona Welsh (Self Help – Business)

Unfortunately, the pot of gold at the end of the rainbow is yet to be found, there doesn't seem to be a Leprechaun smiling at whoever manages to stumble upon this long-famed prize, and as for the money tree, well, it's still as elusive as ever.

From time to time, we all find money hard to come by, and no matter how hard we work, or how much we save, it's likely that there are things we want and need that we can't afford at the present time. Obviously, that doesn't mean that your money situation is going to be difficult all the time, because cash flow ebbs and flows (pardon the pun) as much as anything in life, but finding ways to help it along a little is always a good thing.

The internet has changed so much about our modern-day lives, it is quite hard to think of anything that we don't use an online connection for in some way or another. From booking holidays, doing our grocery shopping, meeting the new Mr or Mrs Right in our lives, or finding a new job, the Internet connects it all. So, taking that thought a little further, can the Internet help us to earn a little extra cash when our flow isn't, well, flowing as fast as we would like?

Of course, it can!

Out Now

Julia's Dilemma– By Lyndsey Carter (Romantic Comedy)

Julia sighed as she stepped onto the escalator. As it moved and took her up, she sighed again. Another boring day and another crammed ride home on a smelly train with no seats. She longed for some excitement, something to shake things up. She was sick of the same old, same old.

Julie boarded the train, already knowing as she craned her neck to scan each corner that there would not be any seats open. Instead, she settled for a hand-hold on the pole near the back wall. But her surroundings ceased to bother her as she stared off into the distance and let her thoughts roam. She looked at the houses she passed and imagined what type of people lived there. The train line ran at the back of the houses giving Julie a view of the garden. Some gardens had washing hanging up; others had kids' toys. Some gardens were overgrown like a mini jungle. It was a little daydream game Julie liked to play when she didn't have a book or paper to read. Soon the passing gardens and motion of the train made her eyes heavy.

Julia fought to keep her eyes open, scared that she would miss her stop. Even after six years of riding the same train back and forth to work, she was still afraid that she would fall asleep and ride until the train reached the end of the line.

Out Now

We also have a selection of Adult Coloring Books to help relax pass the time and de-stress.

Beautiful Illustrations and puzzles in the back for your entertainment.

Visit

www.arylapublshing.com

website to sign up for new release books and free promotions